ONE WASHCLOTH

ONE TOWEL

Katey Geyer Winant

One Washcloth, One Towel

Cover and illustrations by John MacDonald
www.jmacdonald.com

ISBN Number: 978-1-60571-123-2

4869 Main Street
P.O. Box 2200
Manchester Center, VT 05255
www.northshire.com/printondemand

Building Community, One Book at a Time
*This book was printed at the Northshire Bookstore,
a family-owned, independent bookstore in
Manchester Ctr., Vermont, since 1976.*

Printed in the United States of America
using an Espresso Book Machine
from On Demand Books

For Olivia,
Who came back To us in
Time To know and admire him.

always,
Manny

November 2011

For Claudia and Peter

and all of theirs

who are also mine

Author's Note

The numbing agony after losing your
spouse is so overwhelming. It is so
devastating. I still feel shredded. It is my
wish that reading this will be of benefit
to other women and men who have gone
through the long, dark pathway of loss.
My purpose and hope is that there will be
points of identification that will click and
be of comfort. Each of us has our own
story.

A wonderful friend, David Elpern, told me
to get this book on paper. "I want to read
it," he said. I respect him and his intellect
and he pushed me to get going. I am
eternally grateful. I have shared this as well
with Jane Champagne. She is younger and
lost her husband many years ago and way
too soon. She knows all about this black pit
of sadness and I wanted her reaction. She
told me that she cried a great, deep sobbing

kind of cry and she welcomed it. It was a release and she reads the script often. Her response gave me confidence that my goal was on track. Vivienne and Marc Jaffe have been the wind beneath my publishing wings. They never failed to hold my hand and my heart tightly. That they believed in my ability to write was priceless. Marc and my husband supported each other as Marine comrades in the battle of Okinawa in World War II. Help has come as well from the very few others who kindly read my words and told me not to fail in reaching my goal of seeing them in book form. I will forever remain both thankful and overwhelmed by the loyalty and giving from my cherished "believers."

Both John and I were English majors at college. Writing came very easily to him and I admired his way of expression and command of his subjects. I did a great deal of writing at college and planned a life in journalism until he came along and blissfully changed all that. For years, I told him I wanted to write a book. A best seller, naturally. But I never did. How ironic that I have finally put words to paper and they are mostly about losing him.

1.

It is April Fool's Day and I wish with all
my heart that John would peek around the
door and say, "April Fool, I didn't really
die. Here I am and I want to kiss you!"
And that divine man would come to me
and put his arms around me and he would
have that special smile of his and all would
be well.

It seems so unreal to think that over two
years have gone by. I am still curled up
tightly next to him in my mind and heart
and body. Will it ever get less intense? I
don't cry as much or at least like I used
to. Screaming and sobbing and imploring
God to help me. Now, I weep when I see
pictures of or go to places we used to share.
I get "teary" easily and then I swallow hard
and try not to fall into that deep well that I
know so well. Is that improving? I wonder.

For all this time, I have been breathing sort of half way. I cannot seem to take a deep breath. I guess I do when I sleep, but soon after awakening, I can feel the tightness in my chest creeping back. And now, I think I have figured it out. Way, way down deep inside me, there is a deafening, piercing, shattering scream that can't get out. It pushes against my normal inflow of air and I am left with the feeling of holding my breath most of the time. He is so much a part of me. His loss is a stone inside me. I want him near. He always left me breathless, but this isn't the way it should be.

He really did leave me breathless from the moment I saw him coming down the steps at the Cutler's house. A blind date, it was all arranged by lifelong friends. It was soon after the war and we were all so glad to be alive and together. He said, "How do you do," and I think I said, "It is nice to meet you."

It was so nice to meet him. We married ten months later and had sixty-one incredible years together and now he is dead and I can't breathe properly.

2.

"You have Parkinson's." That is what the neurologist said after he watched John walk down the hallway past his office. He was a wonderful doctor and he told us straight out and that was good, for John was a "straight out" type of man. We began to learn what that dreadful disease was all about. He read, he sent for journals and he began to walk a great deal. The signs had been there for some time, but we didn't recognize them. The lack of facial expression at times when all around him were screaming with laughter. I remember looking at him and wondering if he had had a tiny stroke. It wasn't that. And then, he wasn't swinging his arms when he walked like he had always done. He had an easy stride and Marine straightness that was so much a part of him after the rigors of training for and fighting on Okinawa. Buttons became a challenge, but not always, and it was a good amount of time

before he was frustrated by knotting his
tie. He mowed the lawn and dragged brush
and he painted the picnic table and he
kept walking and did exercises. I admired
his tenacity and fell in love with him over
and over again. We didn't talk about the
challenges very much. That wasn't his style
and I respected that.

He wore a tie and jacket to parties and he
was a delightful dinner partner and host.
He was a great father and grandfather
and friend and businessman. He was fun
and fair and patient and decent. He was a
superb lover. No wonder I cannot breathe.

How ironic now to look back on the
failure of his lungs being the cause of his
death. Pulmonary fibrosis and pneumonia
brought him to his knees. My strong
man had to endure a wheelchair and two
oxygen masks twenty-four hours a day.
He needed help and it began to take his
strength a day, an hour, a minute at a time.

And still, he didn't complain. Just once he said, "It doesn't hurt, I'm just sad."

3.

Oh God, it is all so sad. I find myself wondering if I did it all right those last few weeks after we flew him home from the hospital in Denver where they took him when the airline had to divert the plane we were on and take him down for help. He couldn't breathe. He needed oxygen when we reached altitude and he was gasping and they tended him brilliantly. A whole planeload of kind and patient people watched as they saw him safely on the ground and into an ambulance and they waved from the widows of the plane as we pulled away. I thought he would get better. He just hadn't been feeling too well and we decided to go home from California early.

He didn't get better. Not really. We came home on a medical jet and spent ten more days in intensive care at the local hospital. We got him back into the house. There

were two oxygen machines and visiting
nurses and therapists and a trained aide
that came to stay during the night so I
could get sleep for another fourteen-hour
day of taking care of him and his needs.
I thank God that I had the strength and
health that made it possible for me to be
there for him and with him. He was my
man and we were in our house and we both
tried to make it as normal as we could. He
sat in his wheelchair at his desk and did
paperwork and answered the phone and
I really think he felt sure he was on the
mend. He watched the news at night with
a scotch in a glass with a bendy-straw that
he could manage to get in past the mask.
People came to call and we kept a pretty
nice schedule and I was going out of my
mind with worry and sadness and feeling
terribly tired and all along praying that I
would never have to hook up the backup
oxygen tanks if all else failed.

Now, I wonder if I fooled him for a minute.
I doubt it. I tried to look calm and we

carried on and held hands watching the TV in the evening before the aide came. I had to say goodnight and leave to get rest. We knew that. We ached for not being able to end the day next to each other. I hated it. He did too. But, we had no choice. We have no choice. We have no choice that death will come or who will go first or how or when. I try to comfort myself by rejoicing that we do have the choice about how we will lead our lives and with whom we will lead it. I remember vowing at the age of thirteen that I would never proclaim my love to a man unless I really meant it. Never. Ever. And I didn't until three weeks after we met in the hallway of that lovely home in the Berkshires of Massachusetts. I once found a lovely porcelain dresser tray in Williamsburg that says:

> "My heart is fix'd I cannot range,
> I like my choice
> Too well to change."

It is still on his dresser.

4.

I was told that there was no hope for his recovering and that the time had come for Hospice to take over. That, they said, did not mean an imminent time of death. It simply meant that his illness was incurable. I asked for a male nurse because I felt John would like some male help and companionship. The nurse was a pulmonary specialist and he and John got on well. He assured John that he had a lot of patients that he had been with for two years at least, but I don't think that made John feel any better. He hated the idea of signing forms and releases and for him the film that he watched was unsettling. It was a hard time for him and I wanted to scream and hold him and make it all go away. The fact that he was in his home and being tended well was, of course, because of the very care he was being given. But he was getting weaker. The children and grandchildren came and helped and gave him the love and good conversation and understanding he needed so much. They needed the same.

I remember that the laundry was being done, his breakfast was being cooked, he was helped in the shower, the bed was changed, his medicines were laid out. All as it should be. But, something inside me welled up and I stated that I would do the laundry and I would choose his clothes for the next day! My house was being run by other people, my daily life was being run by other people, my husband was being cared for and fed and bathed and organized by other people. I needed them and he needed them and I knew it and deep down I hated it. He was mine, my partner, my love, my soulmate and I couldn't have him to myself anymore. We were not just "us" anymore; we were a household of caring and professional people moving in and out. That delicious aloneness was gone.

And now, the aloneness is what I dread and desire all at the same time. People who know about this are so right. It is the emptiness in the house when you come home, the quiet, the missing warm hug, the voice calling out and the smile and the "Who called?" It is just so damn empty. The rooms and the air and the dark and the bed.

By the same token, I crave the aloneness with him here. After anything that takes me out, I anticipate coming back home. I feel safe here. He is here, I feel so close to him here. I talk to him here and I smile at him here and I flirt with him here and I weep with him here. I still have everything he ever wore or touched or wrote here. Probably there are some who think I am not totally in control, but it is the way I want it. I make no excuses. His closet is not a shrine; it is a place of warmth and strength for me. I can go in and touch a tweed jacket or hold his Marine cap and then I can walk out and close the door and get on with my life. Somehow, I know we both feel nearby.

5.

Four days before John died, our daughter, who had come from California to spend time with her Dad, worked with him arranging his library of Arthuriana. It is a fine collection and he spent years putting it together. We traveled over tors and streams and bridges and the countryside of England in search of the legend. We toured Brittany in France. He wrote scholarly articles and had marvelous correspondence with book dealers all over the world. His library was a constant source of pleasure and interest. He catalogued it carefully.

He sat in front of the shelves in his wheelchair and oxygen masks and patiently pointed to the placement of books. Our grandson had transferred the collection from his study to the library shelves downstairs so that he could be near them. I can see him now. He knew each volume. He polished the very fine leather bound editions so carefully, as weak as he was. He wanted them in perfect order and condition. I wonder if he knew that the end was close. He had made up his mind to get the job done.

I fiddle around making decisions. Not about the color of a room or what to pack or little stuff like that. But, I am very good at swaying back and forth on bigger things. John was patient when I couldn't decide and once gave me advice that has been of great help. He had been offered a position that meant our moving to Washington D.C. A very fine opportunity, but our life in Massachusetts was solid and comfortable. No need to make a change. It was a major decision and a big challenge. "Katey," he said, "we are going to look at this from all angles. Up, down, in, out, good, bad, every way possible. And we will take all the time we need. But, once we have made our decision, we will never look back." We spent the next twenty wonderful years in Alexandria, Virginia.

I don't know just what he was thinking
getting his books in order, but I know he
had a plan and he didn't falter. He stuck
with his decision and I admired and adored
him for it. He taught me so much and
reinforced all the values that I had been
taught. I respected him mightily. I was able
to look at him objectively. I could not love
a man that I could not respect. That came
first and he filled that requisite.

Now, subjectively, that was something
else. He just plain filled all my dreams.
Those first few years living in Manhattan
were everything I could have wished. He
worked the late afternoon shift at The
Associated Press. I would often take a bus
uptown to meet him at 11 at night and we
would go off for a drink with his friends
from the Bureau and would talk about
the news of the day. We slept late and the
city never stopped that wonderful buzz it

has. He was sophisticated and fun and he smoked too much. I guess we all did. It was part of life. Bad stuff and we both gave it up in our sixties. But it stayed with him. I see young people now smoking and I want to go up to them and tell them how foolish they are. I want to tell them that I lost my life's breath from what they are doing.

6.

When I came into our bedroom on the day
he died, I knew something was different.
The aide had gone home, John was
dressed and in his wheelchair and our
son and granddaughter were next to him.
They had let me sleep in a bit. John was
slumped over and not really responding.
We gently tried to help him sit up and then
suggested that he go back to bed and rest
a bit. "Maybe that's a good idea," he said.
Those were his last words. He died five
hours later.

Like millions of fortunate people on this
earth, I had never witnessed the end of
a life before, and now I was nearby my
precious mate and I longed to help him and
I wanted him to know that I was there. The
Hospice nurse came. I remember asking
what the date was. I remember sitting near
him and standing near him and holding

him and it was very important to me to
keep blankets tucked around him. I wanted
him to be warm and safe. He was dying
and I wanted him to be warm.

He told me once that the most important
two things that we do alone in our lives is
to get born and to die. As I watched him,
I knew what he meant. This was his time
and we all wanted to be as quiet and calm
and dignified as we could. I wanted to
scream and call him back all healthy and
handsome and ready for the next project,
but he was dying. His time had come.

It's that breathing thing again. A dying
person begins to breathe deeply and then
irregularly and it comes in intervals and
more shallow. Often the interruptions
make you think it is over. And then it starts
again. I talked to him and told him of my
love and told him it would be all right to
go. I will be O.K. The children and I will
be fine. I thanked him for the fabulous life

he had given to me. I held his arm, I held him, I smoothed his hair.

And then the final breath came and I looked at our son and granddaughter. They had talked to him too. They had stood there bravely and watched a man they loved so much leave this earth. There was no going back. He wasn't going to get better even as hard as he tried to believe he would. He rallied just for a few moments before he died. His color came back, he looked peaceful. I knew it was his goodbye and letting us know he would be fine.

7.

Keeping in mind that he is fine helps. I like to believe that he is breathing freely and walking and even running. He was a star runner when he was young and some of the grandchildren have inherited that ability. They certainly didn't get it from me!

It's funny, but I find that I don't want to run from this grief. I want to understand it. I want to be sensible and methodical and welcoming, just as I wanted to be right after his death. The minister came and we said the Lord's Prayer together over John's body and then he prayed and they all left the room so that I could be alone with my beloved for the last time. I always wondered what one would do when that time came. I really didn't know what to do. I felt at a loss for words. No more to say. We once said that if we couldn't say "I love you" anymore to each other, we had said it enough for three lifetimes. But, I tucked the covers around him again and I told him I loved him and I looked at him. There he was in our bed in our bedroom in our house and we would never live there together again. We had done so well together and could still be doing well, but it was over. It was over. They came and took him away and I watched the hearse go down the driveway and I said goodbye and wished him a wonderful journey.

And then what I have always called "The Procedures of Death" began and it was my turn. I remember wanting the two oxygen tanks that had moaned and puffed twenty-four hours a day for those weeks taken away. I wanted the hospital bed removed. The medicines were removed by the nurse and our bed was put back in its place in our room. The clothes he was wearing were neatly folded. I put his meal tray away. I put his glasses and his watch in a drawer in his desk. I wanted everything back as it had been all those years. I wanted him back. I moved mechanically doing all the things that had to be done. Or at least I thought they had to be done.

I can't remember when I started to sob. There was so much to do. Gathering of family. Friends calling. Funeral to arrange. Food beginning to arrive. Phone ringing, muffled voices answering. I could not have made it without the family in those first days. I suspect the "busyness" is a good thing. It keeps one sane when everything in you is begging and searching for the one you love to be there. Not to be dead.

The end of the day comes. The house is quiet. You hug the pillow and sleep on his side of the bed and you look into the dark and try to see him. And you wonder if there is enough milk in the house and what to wear to the funeral and whether a special friend has been called with the

news. And then you cry into his pillow
and you wonder if you can face the days to
come. You do because you must.

8.

He was so thoughtful about making my
"musts" easier, even after death. There
was a "To-Do" list for KGW in his file
cabinet. It listed everything from collecting
tax information to when to have the oil
changed in the riding mower. God bless
him. He wrote out wishes for hymns
and psalms and the gospel reading at
his funeral service. He cared very much
about his Lord and he had favorite music
and words and he chose carefully. We
carried out his wishes. He was there. His
ashes were in a mahogany case, but to
me he was there in body and soul. We
sang his favorite, "Oh God Our Help In
Ages Past." I could feel him standing next
to me singing without the hymnal. He
knew every verse by heart. His friends,
so many of them, were there and three
Marines came and did everything right
and reverently as they honored him and
presented me with a flag. The service was

right for him and he would have been
proud.

The family all looked so fine and they were
splendid sitting there, each confronting
their own private grief. They adored their
father and grandfather and now they
would have to get on without his smile and
wisdom and laughter and understanding.
He would no longer be able to answer their
questions. We all came to him for answers.
It was rare when he could not help.

I wish now so often that he could send
me messages to answer my questions on
how to get on bravely. I have taken upon
myself to make some decisions that seemed
wise. Being the age I am, I grew up in the
time when women didn't have careers.
We married after the war, had babies and
stayed home and drove car pools and ran
charity bazaar and cleaned the house and
cooked and life was good. Our husbands
worked very hard at their jobs and they

mowed the yard and wrote the checks
and looked out for us. So, deciding to pay
off the mortgage, lock in the oil price for
winter heating, cut down trees and have
the cedar shake roof cleaned all seem
noteworthy to me.

For weeks after he died, there was a crow
that appeared. Sometimes it walked about
and other times it sat on a limb on a maple
tree in the front yard. Usually crows are in
pairs if not crowds, but this one was alone
as far as I could tell. I knew it was John. I
just knew it and I would talk to it before it
flew away. I think I told a couple of people
about it, but not many. I was afraid people
would think I had gone mad with grief. I
had, but I didn't want it to show. Many
months later, when I was walking around
the place, a white butterfly appeared
and hung around for a long time. That
happened with a fly in the kitchen as well.
It let me get very close to it before flying
away.

I had to believe in something. Anything.
I had to get a sign that he was thinking of
me as well. Grasping at straws and clouds
and leaves and scents and sounds are what
I have now, and I will take them any way I
can.

9.

Crows and butterflies aside, it is family
and friends and faith that keep you able
to function properly. A few weeks after
John died, the rector, who had been so
kind before his death and who conducted
his service, asked me to join him for coffee
at the local coffee house. It is always full of
students and locals and a fun place to go.
We settled into a good conversation about
my well-being physically and mentally and
spiritually. None were going full speed, but
that was a given. I remember he asked me
if I was angry with God. I definitely was
not and am not. John had such a deep faith
in God and I have always thought of the
Almighty as a good friend and I knew he
would not have taken him unless it was the
right time. He didn't want my darling and
a cherished member of his flock to agonize
over getting through another day without
breath and hope. I know that John is safe
and at peace. It has taken me a long time to

get up the courage to go to church without him sitting next to me and kneeling beside me. Cowardly, I know, but I didn't want to go to church to cry. I can cry at home. But now, I am going from time to time and I can feel him sometimes and that makes me want to cry. He wouldn't want me to.

Friends swallow you up with kindness and concern and help and food when you lose your husband. They were there immediately. Often, they would come and leave their offering of food or whatever without even coming near me. They just wanted to help. We have all done that, but when you are the recipient, you truly realize that every token is so welcome. They came to the house and to the funeral and they hugged and they cried and they told me how they felt about John. Wonderful words. The letters, nearly three hundred of them, I still have and always will. I want his children and grands and great-grands to know what a respected and special person he was. "True gentleman" was repeated over and over again. He left his mark in so many ways on so many people. He left his mark on me in ways I can't begin to describe, or won't.

Our children, daughter and son, are all grown up and there are dear spouses and grandchildren and great-grandchildren to brag about. In one of the letters that came to me, a colleague of John's wrote, "KateyandJohn was all one word." It was, and now I am reaping the strength and support from those two dear people we created with our oneness. This has been a challenge to each of them in their own way, but their concern for me and my well-being is so apparent. It spoils me. They, along with their families, are in touch and there for me and good about weaving me into their lives and activities and plans. At the same time, I must admit to feeling very lonely when I am with them all at a family gathering at holiday time or whatever. It is when I sit at a Christmas table or a picnic table with them that I miss John terribly. They are all so busy and full of conversation and there is laughter and they fold me in. But, I am so horribly alone. Hard to explain. They are rightfully getting on with their lives together and the young are just getting started on a life that will hopefully be shared and cherished with another. I have had that and am so grateful and I know all that. Yet, I look down the table trying to find him so we could look at each other when it is time to go home together. And then we could talk on the way home about conversations with or plans or hopes or concerns for each one of them.

10.

Hopes and plans are what life is all about.
The good and the bad are the results of
them and that is as it should be. When
you are young and in love there are no
"bads," just good plans and hopes that
last a long time. When you are left alone,
you look back on those times and it helps.
Oh my, how it helps. It has taken me
over two years now, and I am really just
beginning to delve into memories so clear
and cherished. For all this long time, it
has been very hard for me to get a clear
picture of John's face without his two
oxygen masks. There are special pictures
of him in the house that I have had out for
years, so his image is very much around
me, but when I looked for him at times and
places, I couldn't see his handsome face
with a smile on it. I could only see him as
he looked during those last weeks. It was
as if I had lost his "old self," the John that
I knew and lived with and shared with and

laughed with and planned with and talked with all those years. I had lost such vital contact. I couldn't even get through to his real countenance.

And then there is his "spirit." People all around me talk of his spirit being with me and near me and I guess that is true. I say I guess for that is all I can do. Are our memories really what we call "spirit"? Do we conjure up your love's "spirit" by the images that flood? Or is there something that floats close all the time that is really your heart reaching out with an intense yearning? I don't know. Does anyone? Are we supposed to know?

Shortly before he died, we were lying together while he was taking a rest. It was a quiet time and we were close and I told him that I was tortured by his having to deal with such discomfort. His reply was, "Honey, it is what it is." I try to live by that mantra now. I really do. He also was of the belief that death was final and that we would not meet again with wings on. No waking up from death in each other's arms. So, then I am more deeply concerned with the "spirit." I, for one, prefer the waking up in each other's arms. Our daughter said, "Perhaps, it is the first time that Dad was really wrong." None of us know, John among them, what is in store after we die. I do know that when he rallied for those few moments before he died, he looked almost well and happy and anticipatory in the best sense. I truly believe that it was in those moments he was going into a wonderful afterlife. That image remains strongly with me.

Nature has always been a very deep part of my own alliance with God. John and I have been lucky to have homes with a generous amount of acreage around us. We have taken long walks, camped out, waded streams; he built two miles of trails on the property I live on now. He marked with survey tape special trees in the forest, especially oaks, for there aren't very many.

The tapes are still on them and it catches
my breath when I see them. One day,
last spring, I was taking a walk around
the lawns to see how the place had fared
after the winter's toll. We always did that
together and I wanted to carry on the
tradition and I also wanted to know how
the woods looked. It was a sunny afternoon
and as I was walking along the stream,
I looked across into the trees and there,
shining in a ray of sunlight was an orange
tape that he had put there long ago. I had
not ever seen that particular one before.
There it was in the woods, fluttering. It
was as if he was beckoning to me and
my heart stopped and I sat on the bench
nearby and cried my eyes out. It wasn't so
much sad as sweet and so like him.

11.

Trees are so splendid. They are lofty and protective and wonderful to look at. We choose them carefully when we plant them and we admire them and care for them as they mature. In a wooded setting they mingle, and yet each one has its own space and identity. And they can serve as guides along a path or a shoreline.

The two of us loved our yearly trips to Maine. We went to a wonderful place on the shores of Sebago Lake where we had a cabin filled with wood for the fireplace and an ice bucket topped off and ready for our evening drinks when we came in off the lake. The loons and the lake and the good food and the smell of wood fires burning in the morning were a combination that we cherished. The resort was set out on a wooded point on the lake. Huge fir trees canopied the cabins set about. They were our friends. Like the rocks along the shoreline, they never changed.

We both loved to fish. He had a tackle box full of carefully selected lures as well as pliers for the weights and line and band-aids and all the things that he collected over the years that were precious and essential. We fished in a motorboat mostly and he would pull the rope to start the motor and away we would go with high hopes of catching our fill of bass or salmon or whatever. He had the barbs filed off the hooks so that the fish would have a fair chance of wiggling off if we didn't hook it and play it just right for catching fair and square.

But it was the trees along the shoreline that he watched and knew so well. They marked the spots for trolling or where to drop the anchor for still fishing. When we fished from a canoe, he knew his special, friendly trees that guided him into coves

that had been good ones. We took picnic
baskets packed by the lodge and he pulled
into islands for lunch. Mostly, we worked
hard and happily for our catch, but there
were times when we had lunch under those
trees and didn't fish at all for the rest of the
afternoon.

And now I wonder if I have the courage to
go back to that beloved place without him.
It's all part of this grieving and healing
business. Part of me wants to go and
another part pulls back. I know I cannot
return to what we had there together. I
know that. At the same time, would it
soothe me to look out on that lake and look
up at those trees and hear those loons and
smell the wood burning? Is it what I have
to straighten up and do and face, and find
I have climbed over a huge mountain?
Will it teach me to breathe deeply again?
It tempts me and that is a good sign. First
steps are what it's all about and this would
be a really big one.

12.

In those weeks and months following
John's death, I began to keep a list of
all the "firsts" that I had to encounter
alone. It is a dizzying list filled with major
confrontations along with things that
are part of daily life. I have kept the list,
adding to it less as time goes by. I will
share a bit of it for anyone who might find
it recognizable.

There is that first trip to the market. The
house was empty now and all had returned
to their normal routines. The blessed
abundance of food so thoughtfully given
had been gratefully consumed and I was
back to the basic need of milk and eggs
and bread. I have always really enjoyed
marketing. Truly. I like to plan menus
and pick out what I want. There was a
wonderful street market near our flat in

London and it made the whole idea of marketing a fiesta. But, there I was at a standstill. I simply didn't know how to start. One baking potato? Two apples? One lamb chop? I had to leave.

And then there was the first of the many routine appointments. Oil change for the car. Accountant meeting. Arrange for water filter change in the basement. That drive alone to an inn an hour away for a lunch shared annually with friends. Call to arrange the tune-up of the riding mower. Should the chimney be cleaned? Should the septic tank be cleaned? These were not my department. Mine was another and I knew it well.

And then the social scene with houseguests that came from England especially to be with me. A lovely visit and I love them dearly, but so different to be three instead of four. That first cocktail or dinner party to drive to and from alone. Husbands being

so kind about getting your drink. Dear
people asking you to join them for dinner
or a movie and you are the extra one and
you want to pay your own way. All so new.

It took quite a while before I could put on
that first CD and listen to music that had
been our favorites. It damn near killed me
to hear "What Are You Doing The Rest
Of Your Life" or "Misty." His collection
of classical music I put off for a long time.
The plan came to me to work through from
the alphabetical progression on the shelf.
I dreaded Beethoven for he was John's
favorite. I am now up to Sibelius.

So many "firsts," but hearing the peepers
in the pond start their herald of spring
was a dilly. The pond is in the front of the
house near our bedroom window and we
would thrill at that first tiny note each year.
But, the big one, when it all came crashing
down, was the morning those many months
ago when I first changed the linen and only

needed to put out one washcloth and one towel. There it was. My new life.

13.

That towel rack before me said it all. One.
One. Such a simple presentation, yet it
confronted me like a hydra. It still twinges
when I change the linen. Not as much, but
it's there.

The progression of feelings and sensations
and aches and questioning all swirled
around and still do. I finally decided
that I had to settle in my own mind the
distinction between depression and grief.
They were both there and I was awash
in the toll they were taking. Lord knows,
I didn't want to be depressed into an
uncontrollable state of lethargy. I had to
keep functioning for myself and my family
and for him. The crying and deep hurt had
to be grief.

So I looked the definitions up in "The

New Shorter Oxford English Dictionary"
found on a shelf in John's vast collection
of books. His library embodies what he
was. It has been a source of closeness and
comfort to me. I loved watching him hold
a book and turn the pages carefully. He
respected books: he wrote three of them.

Depression: dejection, melancholy, low
spirits. I take from this that depression
is an existing possible condition, a
preponderance that is sparked by an event
that sets it in motion.

Grief: mental anguish, deep sorrow caused
by bereavement, hurt, harm, damage
caused by another. So then, that means to
me an outside force imposed to cause the
sensation of deep hurt.

Mourning: lament, a misfortune, moaning,
a period of showing grief for a loss. This
passes. It is a period. Period.

I got up and got dressed and I showered
and I combed my hair and I answered
the phone and I met with people dealing
with "the estate" and I made decisions
and I think I made sense. So, I am not
in a depression, I said to myself. Please
God, don't let that take over. I was full of
dejection and melancholy and low spirits,
but I could go through the motions and I
could think and I didn't sit in a chair for
hours. My heart sat there, but the rest of
me moved.

So it is grief I am living with. It is still there
after a long time and I now know that it
will always be there. It is part of me. It is
John. It is a reminder of our closeness, in a
way, and I have to look at it and embrace it
for what it is. I will grieve forever. It is the
degree of mental anguish and deep sorrow
that I will have to deal with when it shows
signs of taking over. It is part of the deal.
It is what it is and I must not be afraid
of accepting the role it plays in my daily
living.

14.

Fear is a very large part of this loss/grief
equation. Or at least it is for me. By nature,
I am not a fearless, go-for-it kind of person.
I guess I appear to be pretty under control
and able to take on most any social setting
and situation. If the truth were known,
I am not really all that sure of myself
and I avoid testings that can make me
apprehensive. I don't think I am weak, but
I sure do like it when things go smoothly.
Who doesn't?

John, on the other hand, was fearless. Of
course he feared catastrophic events or
harm to his family or injustice, things like
that. But he went forth with confidence
and tackled what was given to him without
fear as long as he knew he was being fair
and right. I watched him time after time
when challenges came that he had to solve
and it never failed to reach me and teach
me. I felt so protected. It was just the

way he was. He didn't swagger. He just watched over us and in the business world, had to make decisions and carry out tasks that were perhaps sometimes very, very nerve making. I remember a non-somber nor in any way threatening time in Italy when we were on our way to Florence. Probably a silly example, but one that highlights the difference in our approaches. We had rented a car in Pisa and were on the motorway to Florence when a sudden deluge of rain hit us. It was thick and heavy and drenching and it lasted all of about eight minutes. When we pulled off at the exit to Sesto Fiorentino, we came to a gully that had been filled with water and there were cars stalled in the middle, the victims of people trying to make it through. People had gathered on both sides of the road to watch the fun, for drivers were still trying to charge safely to the other side and it was a guessing game. My heart sank, we were so near. How would we get to our destination? No way to turn around. "We're going through," said he. My heart jumped. I was fearful. I could see us stuck in the middle of the lake; I wanted to stay put and safe. We moved forward and entered the water and he kept up a slow, steady speed. We were passed by a car that was racing through and he, of course, scooped water into the grill and came to a stop. We just kept steady-as-you-go and then there was the other side and we pulled out and the people clapped and yelled and waved us on. John turned to me and said, "See, that wasn't so bad, was it?"

But this is bad, this business of being alone and lonely. Thunderstorms and lightning and the coyotes howling at night and darkness outside the windows and long, silent nights don't make me fearful. What I think makes me afraid is the fear of being afraid. Does that make sense? I can't let that happen anymore, for I know what it can do to you. I was fearful, apprehensive may be a better word, for all that long time after the Parkinson's came to live with us.

Sadly, it's big girl time now. I alone am in charge.

15.

For the first twenty years of our marriage, John traveled a great deal. He was a vice-president of an electronics company that had twenty-two factories in America and overseas. Mostly, I stayed home with our children, but one trip especially took us around the world to visit the plants.

We started in Tokyo and our last stop was in London. Our love affair with England began then, way back in the days when "Time, ladies and gentlemen" was called out to warn of the pub's closing at 11 P.M. and Harrods closed at noon on Saturdays. We made trips from time to time for holidays and on one we both conjectured about how marvelous it would be to own our very own flat in London. He made the dream come true. We began to search whenever he was there alone or, when we could, together. No dice. Too big, too little, too expensive, paperwork hurdles. I finally gave up after two years. Not John. He called me from London and said, "I think I have found the right flat. But, I don't want to buy it until you have seen it. I am coming home, but you should get on a plane and look at it and if you like it, buy it."

I wasn't in the habit of buying flats alone, but with his blessing, I got on a plane and flew over. He had it all arranged. Train from Gatwick to London, meet the estate agent, look at the flat and, if all was well, go to our solicitor's office and get the papers in the works. I liked it, went to Mr. Drooglever's office in Cadogan Gardens. He called John. We talked together and rejoiced together and I told him that I was pretty nervous. After the conversation, Mr. Drooglever leaned across his huge desk, took my hand and said, "My dear, you musn't be frightened."

John and I had ten years living in London,
on holidays at first and then for half of each
year after he retired. It was heaven. We
went to the country often to visit friends.
He drove us from Cornwall to Cumbria. I
did not take the wheel. Wrong side of the
road was not for me, but he got us around
with a good degree of ease. Only once, at
Hyde Park Corner in London, did he really
lose his cool. But, that is a formidable
convergence, not for the timid, especially
next to a double-decker bus!

I think of he and I now sitting together
on the #24 bus that took us mostly where
we wanted to go, or riding down that long
escalator in the tube station at Green Park,
or buying books on Charing Cross Road,
or walking through Green Park on Sunday
afternoons. We bought our meat from
Mr. Hart on Tachbrook Street and the
fishmonger on Warwick Way introduced
me to mussels. Primrose plants were
always in the flat. It was a magic time

for us and he was strong and healthy and nothing was ever going to change. I always shed a tear as we lifted off after a stay there to head home. He would take my hand. "We'll be back," he said.

That is one place I can never be without him. That is for sure. He would be on every corner and I am too old to walk about with misty eyes. I have made a firm decision. London is out.

16.

To be precise, I am lonely. I am not alone
in the real sense. I am, adjectively alone,
but I am adverbially lonely. I looked it up.
I have no companion, but I am surrounded
by care and love from those who are family
and those who are friends for keeps. I am
blessed and I know it. I am grateful beyond
measure and I should be spanked if I am
caught whining. As a child, I was never
allowed to whine. I could cry if I was sad
or hurt, but no whining allowed.

So I can't have my way. Not really.
Someone has taken away my nomenclature
on much of the mail that comes. I am
apparently now either Ms. or Mrs.
Kathryn Winant. What took away my
status as being married to John? Where
did Mrs. John H. Winant go? Who makes
these decisions? I don't like it, but there
it is. There are endless things I don't like

about this business of widowhood. I miss buying tickets for two people. I miss making holiday plans and looking at maps and brochures together. I miss calling him on the phone. I miss seeing him in the yard working on a flowerbed. I miss watching him give a speech. I miss meeting him at a restaurant. I miss watching him stoke the fire. I miss sitting next to him in the car. I miss the scent of his shaving cream. I miss his laugh when it was deep and his shoulders shook. I miss him winking at me across the table at a dinner party or across the room. It was a slow wink and it was our own private high sign. It's the missing and the longing and the real effort to get on with life. Good people ask you how you are. They care, they really want to know and you lie and say that you are fine. Most of you is fine so you aren't really lying when you say you are. Your motor is working, but a couple of big parts are not quite in line. Besides, people don't really want to hear your lament and they are quite right in not wanting to do so.

Everybody has a lament. Everybody. Who do I think I am that I am the only one with blood running out of my heart? I look about and admire people much stronger than I. John would not admire me at all for dragging my sadness around. It is up to me. It really comes down to being entirely up to me. I chose not to attend group sessions for help in those first months. I have never been very good at group therapy. So, if that is my choice, then get on with it. It is my turn.

Two days before he died, John said to the nurse, "I don't want to do this anymore." So like him. He had given it his all. He was tired beyond compare. He knew that recovery was not even on the page. He had been with all of his family within the holidays. I am a rotten actress and I guess there was no way for him not to see the sadness and worry on my face. He had lost charge of taking care of himself. So, he simply let that brave body give in and

do what it had to do. That took enormous
courage and determination on his part. I
know for sure that it did.

So, I had jolly well better take a page out
of his book, his Bible, and do the very same
with whatever is in store for me. For better
or for worse and for whatever, give it all I
have got.

will always be there. I know it. I am doing
my best to walk with balance to its step.

Yesterday, Mr. Whitman came to pick
up the mower to get it tuned up for the
summer. I have taken my winter coats to
be cleaned and ready for summer storage.
The snow is almost gone and the streams
are running full and fast. The children and
their families all seem to be doing well.
For a little while, I opened the windows in
the house after the long winter to let some
fresh air move in a bit. I had some friends
in for a light supper last night. It is quiet
cleaning up alone without his help, but
it is done. Two crocuses are up. A crow
was in a tree along the driveway when I
went down for the paper this morning. I
can hear frogs croaking in the pond now.
The peepers will surely be coming soon
to sing their lovely song of new life and
new season. A beginning for them. I have
almost decided to write to the lodge in
Maine and request their brochure.

Katey Geyer Winant was born and raised
in South Bend, Indiana. She received
her B.A. degree from Skidmore College
where she was on the staff of the literary
magazine and editor of the yearbook. Her
creative writing interest was nurtured there
and she wrote for the local newspaper as
well.

"Sentences are like flower arrangements,"
she says. "Each word should be chosen and
combined with others to create a balanced
and appealing presentation. It's fun and the
resulting effort should be a pleasure to the
eye."

She lives in the Berkshires in Western
Massachusetts. *One Washcloth, One Towel* is
her first published work.

Cover design and illustration by John
MacDonald, friend, neighbor and artist.